incredible readable rhymes by Steven James

# Believe It!

Bible basics that won't break your brain

Illustrated by Jared Lee

**Standard**
PUBLISHING
CINCINNATI, OHIO

## Hey, everyone!

Ever since the early days of the church, Christians have looked for ways to clearly explain their beliefs and take a stand against false teachings. The rhymes in this book will remind you what Christians believe, and help you explain these beliefs to others.

Some people think learning about God is boring, but the Bible is the most alive book in the world! So, the rhymes in this book are fun to read and easy to remember.

*I'd like a rhyme that's credible,*
*Believable and readable.*
*   (I do not need one edible*
*   But truthful? Yes indeedable!)*
*'Cause God is so incredibly beyond what is conceivable,*
*   It's time to read a rhyme about eternal life receivable!*

I hope this book will bring you closer to God and help you experience the joy and wonder of being best friends with Jesus. Read on! And enjoy!

For God's kids everywhere,
Steven James

**Special thanks from Steven James**
Many people gave me thoughtful and helpful suggestions for this manuscript. Special thanks go out to Jerry Williams, Penny Kilgore, Tom Oyler, Dave McAuley, Kurt Jarvis, Aaron Wymer, Trinity Huhn, Ariel Huhn, Liesl Huhn, Mark Steiner and Rob Forseth for their encouragement, ideas, and input.

**Dedication**
This book is dedicated to Vicki DeYoung, a woman who cares deeply about children and has dedicated her life to sharing God's love with the next generation.

# Table of Contents

# Introduction

This book is quite different
From others you've read,
(Yes, even those tales
For tucking in bed)
For this book is packed
From beginning to end,
With unbeatable teachings
That *you* can defend!
    (And incredible rhymes
    You can read to a friend!)
These rhymes are not musty,
Or dusty, or moldy!
They are not confusing,
Accusing, or scoldy!

They're simply new ways
To explain what is certain;
To let in the light
And pull back the curtain
So you can see clearly
What God wants to show,
And believe in the message
He wants you to know.

    Then you can remember
    And simply explain
    The most vital teachings
    The Scriptures contain!

*So flip over the page*
*And prepare to get started,*
*Reading rhymes of the truths*
*That our God has imparted!*

CHECK it out then CHECK it off...

○ Read Proverbs 2:3-5

# Part 1

# The Best Book of All

# Why is the Bible special?

The Bible is cool!
It's awesome and true.
It's God's special message
Recorded for you.
It's different from all other
Books on the shelf
'Cause God was the author
And wrote it himself!

It wasn't "made up"
Like a legend or fable.
It's *totally true*
Because God isn't able
To make a mistake
Or let errors slip in.
You can trust what it says
Through thick and through thin!

So what's in the Bible?
What does it contain?
God's plan of salvation
Made simple and plain!
  With parables, poems,
  And prayers you can pray,
  And tales of heroes
  Who lived far away!
  The Bible predicts
  What the future will bring,
  And it even includes
  A few songs you can sing!
  It has stories and warnings
  Of what not to do,
  And the best of all news—
  God came to save *you*!

CHECK it out then CHECK it off...

○ Read Psalm 119:16
○ Read 2 Peter 1:20, 21

# Why is the Bible useful?

Two parts to the Bible—
The Old and the New.
Each part is still Bible.
Each part is still true.
Each part's called a *Testament*,
And to help you keep track,
Remember: "Old in the front
And New in the back!"

There are sixty-six *books*
In the two parts combined,
And if you counted each *chapter*
In the Bible you'd find
One thousand, one hundred and eighty-nine!
   (And that's more than I'd care
   To count at one time!)

There are *thirty-one thousand*
Verses for learning,
Correcting, directing,
Perfecting, discerning,
And telling of God
And His wonderful ways,
Helping us, teaching us
Each of our days,
Guiding and leading,
Improving our choices,
Our actions,
    Our thoughts,
    And the use of our voices!

CHECK it out then CHECK it off...

○ Read Psalm 25:5
○ Read Psalm 119:11
○ Read 2 Samuel 7:28
○ Read 2 Timothy 3:16

## How many books did God write?

The Bible's complete
And it shouldn't be changed,
Rewritten, reworded,
Rephrased, rearranged.
Never add your own teachings
Or take some away.
This *one* book contains
All that God wants to say!
    Of all of the writings
    That people might write,
    There is only one writing
    That's totally right!
    There is only one Bible,
    One book that is holy.
    (It's like playing hockey—
    You get only one goalie!)

Though some folks deny it
And make quite a fuss,
The Bible's the *only* book
God wrote for us.
   (And though His opponents
   Have tried hard to ban it,
   God's Word keeps on spreading
   All over the planet!)

CHECK it out then CHECK it off...

○ Read Revelation 22:18, 19

# What should I remember about the Bible?

The truth of the Bible
Is always the same—
God forgives sin,
Takes our guilt and our shame!
For its life-giving words
Touch souls that are dead,
And divinely revive 'em,
Leaving live ones instead!

If it helps you remember,
Just say this refrain:
    "The Bible's from God
    And will always remain!
    God speaks through the Bible—
    Each word and each page—
    And His message extends
    To the end of the age!"

Yes, the Bible will change you
In big ways and small.
It's the best book you'll find
And the greatest of all!

CHECK it out then CHECK it off...

○ Read Psalm 119:89
○ Read John 20:31
○ Read 1 Peter 1:24, 25

**17**

# Part 2

# Our God Is the Greatest!

# Who is God?

God is a spirit,
Not a "he" or a "she"
Or an "it" or a "them"
Or a "you" or a "me."
We call God a "he,"
Though He isn't a man.

(I guess you could say
It's a part of the plan
'Cause through all of the Bible,
God's never called "she."
But He is called our Daddy,
And a Dad is a "he!")

So, who *is* this spirit,
And what can He do?
And how does God differ
From me and from you?

Well, God isn't stuck
In just one single place.
He can travel through time!
He can travel through space!
In the blink of an eye,
In a flash He could be
Anywhere, anyplace
In the whole galaxy!
    (Now you have to admit,
    It would be pretty neat
    To be able to walk
    Without using your feet!)

And He's also invisible!
He doesn't need clothes!
He doesn't have eyeballs,
A tongue, or a nose!
    It's cool that God's different
    From you and from me
    'Cause God is a spirit
    That no one can see!

CHECK it out then CHECK it off...

○ Read Psalm 139:8-10
○ Read John 4:24

# What is God like?

Our God is so generous,
Giving, and fair.
He is helpful and kind,
And He'll always be there
To come when you need Him,
To hug when you're sad.
He's better than even
The very best dad!
He's cooler than cool
And He's better than good!
Always doing precisely
The things that He should.

He's patient and faithful,
Devoted and true,
And loving. There's nothing
Our God wouldn't do
To give you a mansion
In heaven above.
Oh, our God is packed full
Of the most perfect love!

CHECK it out then CHECK it off...

○ Read Deuteronomy 32:4
○ Read 1 John 4:8

# What is God's love like?

God's love doesn't slip
Or stutter or stop.
His love will not fade
Or fail or flop.
His love doesn't cool,
Burn out or get cold.
His love doesn't waver,
Get tired or old.
His love can't be shattered
Or splintered or lost.
It will not be scattered
Like smoke or exhaust.

His love doesn't melt
Like a field full of snow.
God's love will be with you
Wherever you go!
God's love lasts forever;
You can't find its end.
And it's never used up
'Cause He's that kind of friend!

CHECK it out then CHECK it off...

○ Read 1 John 4:9, 10
○ Read 1 John 4:19

# Does God still love me when I'm bad?

Nothing can sever
God's kids from His love.
No nothing, not ever
On earth or above!

Not the depths of the sea,
Or the ends of the sky!
Not the dead or the living,
The low or the high!
Not the future, the past!
Not time and not space!
Not angels, or demons,
Or an alien race!

'Cause nothing can sever
God's kids from His grace!
(Or hide us forever from seeing His face!)

He won't love you less
When you fail to obey
Or ask you to leave Him
And just go away.
So when you discover
You've done something bad,
Don't worry! God loves you!
Be happy, not sad!
    You can trust His forgiveness;
    It's all that you need.
    His love is one hundred percent guaranteed!

CHECK it out then CHECK it off...

○ Read Romans 8:38, 39

# Does God ever make mistakes?

God is righteous—which means
That He does what is right.
God is holy—as pure
As a snowflake is white.
Like laundry that's clean
And not dirty or stinky,
Without any stains
That look muddy or inky!

He's pure! God is pure
Without any mistakes!
Always perfectly doing
What He undertakes.
He does everything right!
He does everything well,
Without ever complaining
Or having to yell!

He's kept every promise
That He's ever spoken.
(He's made quite a few,
And not one has been broken!)
For God tells the truth
And He never tells lies.
His Word is sincere—
With no tricks or disguises.
    (Though He sometimes reveals it
    In ways that surprise us!)

CHECK it out then CHECK it off...

○ Read Deuteronomy 32:4
○ Read Psalm 18:30

## Does God die?

Our God lives forever,
Yet never gets older.
He never gets hotter.
He never gets colder.
He never gets sick
With the measles or mumps.
God doesn't get "boo-boos,"
Or "owies," or bumps.
He never has fevers
Or pimples to pop.
  He doesn't sleep late
  Or vacation atop
  A faraway, ritzy resort in the sky.
  God always, oh always,
  Is very close by!

He's as close as your nose
And as near as your ear!
So you're never alone
And have nothing to fear.
We say He's "eternal"
'Cause He's always around—
In the future,
The past,
In the sky,
On the ground.
You can never escape Him;
It's good news to know
That He'll already be there,
Wherever you go!

CHECK it out then CHECK it off...

○ Read Psalm 90:2
○ Read John 1:1, 2

## Does God sleep?

God doesn't need sleep.
He's awake every day.
No napping, or snoozing,
Or snoring away!
Here's one way to say it.
Here's what we believe:
*"God doesn't play hooky*
*Or need a sick leave.*

"He'll never get tired,
Or move far away.
Our God doesn't change,
And we like it that way
'Cause He's always on duty
Working just like He should,
Making sure even bad things
Work out for our good!"

 CHECK it out then CHECK it off...

○ Read Psalm 121:3
○ Read Romans 8:28
○ Read Hebrews 13:8
○ Read James 1:17

# How strong is God?

God is way beyond perfect
And better than best.
He could pass any quiz!
He could ace any test!
    He knows all there is
    Or could ever be learned,
    And He owns everything
    That could ever be earned!

God doesn't eat food
Or need water to drink.
There's no limit to how many
Thoughts He can think!
He's bigger and stronger
Than anything, ever!
To Him a big mountain's
As light as a feather!

He's the King of the earth!
And the King of the sky!
And no one could hurt Him,
However they try!
No problem's too big
And no problem's too small.
Since God is *almighty*,
He'll conquer them all!

 CHECK it out then CHECK it off...

○ Read Psalm 24:10
○ Read Psalm 28:8
○ Read Isaiah 43:15
○ Read Luke 1:37

# How many Gods are there?

We believe in one God,
Never two or a dozen.
Just one God alone,
With no uncle or cousin
Or grandma or sister
Or mother or brother.
Just one God alone—
One God and no other.
It's simple to know
And it's simple to say:
    "There's only one God
    Who is living today.
    He's been around always,
    And always will be.
    He's the first and last—only—God,
    We guarantee!"

God works in three ways
And has three jobs to do,
Though it might seem confusing
To me or to you.

Sometimes we say God
Has three *Persons* inside Him.
    (Not persons like us—
    It's just a way to describe Him;
    And we say "Three-in-One"
    'Cause you can't just divide Him!)

He's not pieces or parts
Of a puzzle so strange.
God isn't a riddle
That you rearrange.
The three Persons together
Are really the same.
There's only one Holy One,
And *God* is His name!

CHECK it out then CHECK it off...

○ Read 1 Corinthians 8:6
○ Read Ephesians 4:6

# How can God be "Three-in-One"?

A fire has *heat*
And *coals* and a *flame*—
Three *parts* to a fire,
Yet no one would claim
That three fires are burning
When you only have one,
Or that nothing was burning
When your marshmallow's done!

Do you see how this picture
Of flame and a fire
Can teach us about
The one God we admire?
There's only one fire,
Not three, and not two.
There's only one God
Who loves me and loves you—
The Father, the Spirit,
And Jesus the Son,
All working together
To get the job done.
　　For each of the three
　　Plays a wonderful part
　　In heating the coldest
　　And frigidest heart.

Though mysterious, marvelous,
Fantastic, and odd,
Our God has three Persons,
And each is still God!

CHECK it out then CHECK it off...

○ Read Matthew 28:19

# What should I remember about the "Three-in-One"?

So, here's my confession,
Here's what I believe.
I've nothing to hide
And no card up my sleeve:

*"I believe in the Father,*
*The Spirit, the Son—*
*One God in three Persons,*
*Yet still only one.*
*And though in my heart*
*It's a truth that I know,*
*It's tough to imagine,*
*Explain, and to show*
*How three can be one*
*And yet one can be three?!*
*It's exciting!*
    *Inviting!*
    *A divine mystery!*
*(That's who God says He is,*
*And that's OK by me!)"*

Now it's time to look closely
At God's work because
Each Person of God
Has a job that He does!

CHECK it out then CHECK it off...

○ Read Exodus 3:14

# Can I call God my Father?

Long ago you were born
To your mom and your dad
As a cute little lassie
Or handsome young lad.
(Yes, it's true, you were born,
Don't believe Uncle Mork,
No one hatches from cabbage
Or drops from a stork.)

Well, here's something new
That you may not have heard:
God's children are born
Of both *water* and *Word*!
For when you trust Jesus
To forgive all your sins,
Then life in a special
New family begins—
God adopts *you*
As a child of His own,
One He chose and He knows
And He'll never disown!

The Word gives you life,
If you trust when you hear it—
Born once to your parents,
Then again by the Spirit!
And from that moment on
'Til forever is done,
You've a Father in heaven
And a brother, His Son!

CHECK it out then CHECK it off...

○ Read Psalm 68:5
○ Read Psalm 103:13
○ Read John 3:5
○ Read 1 John 3:1

# What does God the Father do?

Our God does what any
Good Father would do:
He loves, He protects,
And He takes care of you.
  Sometimes giving rules
  That will keep you from harm,
  Or calming your heart
  When it's full of alarm,
  Or being close by
  When you feel all alone,
  Or punishing conduct
  He doesn't condone;
  Yet, forgiving you
  Every time you disobey,
  And inviting you back
  When you wander away.

He won't ever leave you.
He won't change His name.
Even if you don't listen,
He'll love you the same.
Yes, *even* when you behave
Nasty or bratty,
He'll always stick with you.
He'll still be your Daddy.

CHECK it out then CHECK it off...

○ Read Psalm 18:2
○ Read Psalm 86:15

## What should I remember about God the Father?

Here is a little
Confession to say,
To clear any doubt
Or confusion away:

*"I believe in my*
*Heavenly Father above,*
*The source of all life!*
*The source of all love!*
*He adopted me into His family,*
*And so He will not, He cannot,*
*Desert me, I know.*
*My faith gives me hope*
*Even when I am sad,*
*For I know that my God*
*Is my Heavenly Dad!"*

Some folks may say I'm fanatical,
But I just call it radical!
'Cause now on high,
I've got a guy
I call my Heavenly *Dad-i-cal*!

CHECK it out then CHECK it off...

○ Read Romans 8:15
○ Read Ephesians 1:4, 5

# Part 3

## it's a Girl Thing

### Christ, Savior the World!

# Is Jesus God?

*Jesus!*
Now I know
That's a name that you've heard.
But before He was born,
Jesus' name was "The Word."
And He ruled all there is,
Like a King in the sky!
But He knew He'd be coming
To earth, and here's why:
Long ago,
Long before
This little planet was formed,
Before the stars twinkled
Or the sky ever stormed,
Our God had a dream,
A magnificent plan,
To bring peace to people
By becoming a man!

So He took off His robes.
He set down His crown,
He arose from His throne
And agreed to come down.
And when no one was looking,
It finally occurred—
The Word came to earth
So the Word could be heard!

CHECK it out then CHECK it off...

○ Read Matthew 16:15, 16
○ Read Luke 22:70
○ Read John 1:1-3

## Was Jesus human?

The Word poured himself
Into a baby so small.
He was born in a stable
And slept in a stall.
He was *God* wrapped in *Man*
Like words wrapped in a song.
　　So helplessly human,
　　Yet all-mightily strong!
　　(And pleasing to God
　　'Cause He never did wrong.
　　He's the only one ever
　　To live without sinning,
　　Even though He was tempted
　　From the very beginning!)

Our God, our Creator,
Was born and became
A baby called *Jesus*—
For that was His name!
Not just God, not just Man,
Not just one or the other,
But *both* Man and God!
Both our Savior and brother!
Both human and holy,
A guy and a God!
How strange! How amazing!
How unusually odd!
   (I'm glad He was human
   And not tuna or cod.)

CHECK it out then CHECK it off...

○ Read Philippians 2:5-8

# What did people think of Jesus?

Jesus grew from a child,
To a teen, to a man.
Then the day finally came
When His mission began.
He told all His followers
Why He had come.
But they thought He was crazy!
They thought He was dumb!
No one knew what to think
Or just how to respond.
He did wonderful wonders
Without waving a wand!

*"He heals the sick!*
*He makes blind people see!*
*Does anyone know*
*Who this healer could be?*
*He walks on the water!*
*Makes demons obey!*
*He controls the weather,*
*And some people say*
*He does magic with food,*
*Making much more to munch.*

*He fed a huge crowd*
*With a little boy's lunch!*
*He talks to the dead*
*And then makes them alive!*
*Could it be the Messiah*
*Has finally arrived?"*

(Though the teachers and preachers
Were a little befuddled,
And they got God's predictions
Mixed up and all muddled,
At least they remembered
God's promise to send
A Savior who'd set them
All free in the end!)

CHECK it out then CHECK it off...

○ Read Mark 4:35-41
○ Read Mark 6:30-44
○ Read Mark 8:22-26
○ Read John 11:1-44

# What did Jesus do?

Jesus helped and He healed.
He showed kindness and love.
He told stories of home
And His kingdom above.
He talked as if God
Were His Daddy and Father.
It made quite a stir!
Yes, it caused quite a bother!

The leaders all hated
This talk about "Dad"!
They thought it was wrong
And they thought it was bad.
So they schemed up a scheme
And got people to lie.
And they told Jesus,
   *"For breaking our laws you must die!"*

They threatened Him, hurt Him,
And just wouldn't quit!
But He never complained.
No, not one little bit,
Even though He was laughed at
And spit at
And hit!

Then Jesus hung high
On a cross and He sighed.
And He said, "It is finished."
And then,
Jesus died.

CHECK it out then CHECK it off...

○ Read Mark 15:16-20
○ Read John 19:30

# Did Jesus stay dead?

For three days it seemed
Like He'd never arise.
Could His talk and His promises
All have been lies?
Could Jesus have lost?
Could the devil have won?
No! The story of Jesus
Had only begun!
For even before
The breaking of dawn,
When they went to the grave
They found Jesus was gone!

They were stunned!
They were startled!
And shocked with surprise!
They blinked and they wondered
And rubbed at their eyes!
Then an angel appeared
And the people soon learned
That their friend wasn't dead,
But instead had returned!
Jesus, our Hero,
Did just what He'd said!
He died and then came back to life
From the dead!
　　He did it to rescue us all from our sin.
　　God's kingdom was opened
　　So all could come in!

CHECK it out then CHECK it off...

○ Read Romans 1:4
○ Read Romans 8:11

# What should I remember about Jesus?

So, here is a verse
To recite and to learn:

*"Jesus is God*
*And He's gonna return.*
*He died to forgive.*
*He died in our place.*
*To arrange the exchange*
*Of our guilt for His grace!*

*"And He rose from the dead*
*To make sure we would know*
*That all who believe*
*Will most certainly go*
*To a heavenly home,*
*To a most perfect land*
*Where Jesus is Lord*
*And rules all by His hand.*
*For only through faith*
*In Him and no other*
*Can heaven be home*
*And He be your brother!"*

CHECK it out then CHECK it off...

 ○ Read Matthew 26:64
○ Read 2 Timothy 1:10

# Part 4

# The Holy Spirit's Many Jobs

# Who is the Holy Spirit?

Sometimes people call Him
The "Most Holy Ghost,"
But He doesn't haunt houses
Or ships on the coast.
He doesn't say "Boo!"
Or dress up in a sheet,
But He moves like the wind
On invisible feet!

He's the Author!
The One who told men
What to write.
He guided their work
To make sure it was right.
And the Bible turned out
Just the way that He planned.
So perfect! So holy!
So gloriously grand!

He's God and He's mighty!
Lighting hearts that are dim!
The Father sent Jesus
And Jesus sent Him!

CHECK it out then CHECK it off...

○ Read 1 Corinthians 2:13
○ Read 2 Peter 1:20, 21

# What is the Holy Spirit like?

The Spirit has feelings.
He grieves and He cries
Over sin, but rejoices
When we realize
That living for God
Is the best way to go,
And letting Him guide us
Will help us to grow!

Sometimes He's a whisper
Deep down in your heart.
Sometimes He's the courage
To make a fresh start.
Sometimes He's the wonder
At all God has done,
And sometimes the mystery
Of knowing God's Son.

But always, oh always,
He'll brighten and cheer!
He'll give strength and courage
And clear away fear!
And help every Christian
Be bold and be brave
When sharing the news
That Christ came to save!

CHECK it out then CHECK it off...

◯ Read John 14:26

# What does the Holy Spirit do?

Like a friend He is there
To support and assist!
Like a trainer He helps us
Grow strong to resist
    The temptations of Satan
    Even when they persist!

He's a guide through the jungles
Of worry and doubt;
A landlord who'll never
Kick anyone out;
A teacher of truth
Who explains and advises;
A detective uncovering
Our masks and disguises;
    (So He knows all our secrets,
    Even those deep inside us!)

He's counselor who listens
And comforts and cares;
And a gardener who digs up
And daily prepares
Our hearts to receive
All the fruit that He shares!

He's a janitor cleaning!
Scrub! Scrub!
And splish splash!
Sweeping dirty ol' thoughts
From our minds to the trash!
  (And He's even a helper
  Who helps us to pray,
  Though our mouths may not know
  All the right words to say!)

But His biggest, best job
Is to help people learn
That getting to heaven
Isn't something you earn!
  It's a gift that is given
  And offered for free
  When the Gospel is shared
  With you or with me!

CHECK it out then CHECK it off...

○ Read Galatians 5:16
○ Read Romans 8:26
○ Read 1 Corinthians 2:12

# What else does the Holy Spirit do?

What else does He do?
And where does He live?
He lives inside Christians
And helps them to give
Away *spiritual* gifts
Like leading and preaching,
And caring and serving
And spiritual teaching!
    (Not gifts like a doll
    Or a truck or a toy,
    But presents like kindness
    And patience and joy!)

And the reason He gives
All those presents away
Is because of His work
And the role that we play
In offering others
The wonder of *grace*!
*Our gifts should be shared*
*With the whole human race!*

For the Spirit renews
(Though the devil accuses)
Whenever you trust
And stop making excuses!
    When you ask for the Spirit,
    God never refuses!

CHECK it out then CHECK it off...

○ Read Galatians 5:25

## What should I remember about the Holy Spirit?

The Spirit is changing me,
Making me holy—
Though not all at once;
It all happens slowly.
He comforts believers
On days they are sad,
And reminds them
They have a great heavenly Dad!
And He gets in your thoughts
And He gives them a prod,
    When you turn from,
    Or drift off,
    Or wander from God.

Like the warmth of the sun
On a cold winter day,
He heats up our hearts
When He comes in to stay
As He fills us with hope
And melts sadness away!

Yet, with all of His jobs,
And with so much to do,
The Spirit of God
Cares most about *you*.
Like a spiritual vitamin
Loaded with power,
The Spirit gives spiritual
Strength every hour!

So relax and don't worry!
You're not on your own!
When God lives inside you,
You're never alone!

CHECK it out then CHECK it off...

○ Read Ephesians 3:16
○ Read John 16:13

# Part 5

# All About Creation

# Who made the world?

Long, long ago,
Before time had begun,
There was nothing but God—
No moon and no sun,
No sky and no stars,
No earth and no sea.
No, nothing existed . . .
'Til He said, *"Let there be!"*
 And as God said the words,
 It all came about—
 For the world He'd dreamed of
 Came whirling out!

*"Let there be!*
*Let there be!*
*Let there be!"*
*And there was!*
Hyenas to laugh
And mosquitoes to buzz,
Eagles to soar
In the newly made sky,
Burrowing worms
And wet octopi,

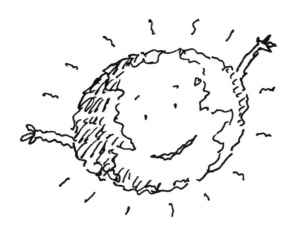

Gators to tromp
On the swampy shores,
Stomping gorillas
And tigery roars.

Light in the darkness!
Life on the land!
*WHAMO! KA-BLAMO!*
The world began!

CHECK it out then CHECK it off...

○ Read Genesis 1:1
○ Read Psalm 33:9

# What else happened at creation?

There were animals everywhere
Swinging and flipping,
And worming and squirming,
And springing and slipping,
And gliding and sliding,
And crawling and creeping,
And walking and stalking,
And falling and leaping,
And bouncing and pouncing,
And slithering down,
And galloping, jumping,
And bumping around!

There were oceans and rivers
And mountains and hills
For furry long legs,
And flippers, and gills!
Now squid in the ocean!
Now plants on the ground!
The first ever smell,
And the first ever sound!

Sunlight and seaweed
And mountains and air!
The hippo! The puppy!
The Kodiak bear!
    It musta been cool!
    It musta looked weird!
    Where nothing had been,
    A whole world appeared!

CHECK it out then CHECK it off...

○ Read Genesis 1:20
○ Read Genesis 1:24

## Where did people come from?

When He'd finished creating
This big earthly ball,
Making all that there is
Out of nothing at all,
God came down to visit
The world that He'd made
Where all of the animals
Frolicked and played.
And He planted a garden
To blossom and bud,
And He made the first man
From a handful of mud.
Then He fashioned a woman
To stand by his side—
    Adam, the groom,
      And Eve, the first bride!

Yes, the Bible explains
Humans weren't a mistake.
(No one climbed from the slime
Of some long ago lake.)
We were formed!
We were fashioned!
We were specially made
To enjoy God forever—
    Never being afraid;
    Living free in a world
    Where His love is displayed!

CHECK it out then CHECK it off...

○ Read Genesis 1:26
○ Read Genesis 2:7
○ Read Genesis 2:21, 22

# Why are people special to God?

God made us to know Him
And rule His creation
With wisdom, compassion,
And great celebration!
He gave us His *image*—
It's kind of a riddle—
>     We're not look-alikes,
>     But we're like Him a little!

We know what it means
To forgive and to care,
To show mercy and justice.
We know how to share.
We can think! We can love!
We create and we dream.
We plan and we feel
Both regret and esteem!
We wonder. We hope.
We desire. We know.
We listen and reason.
We learn and we grow!

We're designed by the Master!
He pulled out the stops;
Making people more special
Than creatures or crops!

CHECK it out then CHECK it off...

○ Read Genesis 1:27

# Is the universe perfect?

The world was *so good*—
Just the way God intended.
But then people sinned
And the harmony ended.
'Cause the wrong things we think,
And the wrong things we say,
And the wrong things we do,
All affect us each day.

So, now that first likeness
Isn't all that it was.
God's image in us
Has been spoiled because
We've disobeyed God
And we've chosen to sin.
By rejecting what's right
We let evil creep in.
　　And His image gets harder
　　And harder to see
　　'Cause we're less like the likeness
　　God made us to be!

Now, the world's wearing out
And it's groaning because
The universe longs
To be back like it was!
    (Yet, God holds it tight
    By His strength and His might,
    To make sure things like gravity
    Keep working right.)
And the galaxy waits
To gleam like a jewel
    On the day of the glorious
    Galactic renewal!

Yes, one day all good
Will be finally restored
When believers go home
To be with the Lord!

CHECK it out then CHECK it off...

○ Read Romans 8:19-22

## Are demons real?

Long ago, before people
Were even created,
Our God made the angels.
But one of them hated
Being less than the best,
So to prove he was right,
    He rebelled with his friends
    Against God, the Almighty!

He tried to take over
God's heavenly throne!
He wanted to take it
And make it his own!
But God didn't like that,
Not one little bit.
So He sent faithful angels off
Lickety-split
Who fought with the rebels
And made them all go
    Out of heaven and sent them
    To earth down below!

And that's where they live now.
Among us. Unseen.
Evil demons who love
To be hurtful and mean.
Their leader is Satan.
He's the meanest and worst.
     (Though he used to be beautiful,
     Now he is cursed!)

And ever since then
He's been looking around
For folks to devour
And folks to drag down
Into darkness, and sadness,
And anger, and sin.
Don't listen to demons!
Don't ever give in!
'Cause they don't tell the truth,
They just lie and deceive,
Trying daily to harm
All of those who believe!

CHECK it out then CHECK it off...

○ Read Isaiah 14:12
○ Read 1 Timothy 4:1

# What are angels like?

So, if demons are bad
And lead people astray,
Then what about angels?
What role do *they* play?
Do they just fly around
With their fluffy white wings,
With a halo and harp,
Slowly strumming the strings?
    Not quite. That's not right.
    They're not little fairies.
    (I don't care what it says
    In those old dictionaries.)

For angels aren't fragile,
Or frail, or small.
They're strong and they're mighty!
And they're probably taller
Than even the biggest guy
You've ever met!
Yes, angels are warriors
Who won't ever let
The forces of evil close in
Or take over.
    They're better protectors
    Than guard dogs named Rover!

And angels don't die.
They don't marry or mate,
So they're never distracted
By getting a date.
    (Or hugging or smooching
    Out there by the gate!)

We don't pray to angels.
They don't answer prayer.
We trust that God rules them
And know that they're there—
As they honor their King,
And obey His commands—
To make sure that His kingdom
Won't shrink, but expands!

CHECK it out then CHECK it off...

○ Read Matthew 18:10
○ Read Matthew 22:30

# What should I remember about angels and demons?

Demons bring doubt
And destruction and pain—
Wanting nothing but sadness
And guilt in your brain!
And though for awhile
They're still free to roam,
No demon will dwell
In a heavenly home.
For one day they'll fall
In a fiery lake
And suffer forever
Without any break.
     (It know it sounds scary,
     But those who love sin
     And hate God and hate heaven
     Will all be thrown in!)

And angels?
Each day they obey as they should;
Fighting mightily onward,
Defending what's good
As they guard and they serve
And surround and protect
All Christians from demons,
Just like you'd expect.

So we thank God for loving
His children and sending
Those powerful warriors
For guarding, defending,
And serving each person
Who trusts in His Son.
*For this war against demons*
*Will one day be won!*

CHECK it out then CHECK it off...

○ Read 1 Peter 3:22

# Part 6

# Sin and Salvation

## What is sin?

If the way that we act
And the things that we say
Could be changed into clothes
That we wear every day,
They wouldn't be spotlessly
Clean or all bright
Because we so often
Don't do what is right.
For even the very best
Deeds that we do
Look muddy and grungy
And stained through and through
To the God who is perfect
And holy and true!

(And if those are the very best
Clothes we can bring,
It's like wearing dirty laundry
In front of our King!)

'Cause the Bible says breaking
God's law is called "sin."
And sin makes us dirty
*Inside* of our skin,
   So we need to be washed
   And scrubbed from *within*!
No matter how nice
It may seem at the time,
Every sin makes your soul
All covered with grime.
And the cleaning you need
Is the cleaning God gives
When He cleanses your soul
By the sin He forgives.

CHECK it out then CHECK it off...

○ Read Psalm 51:7
○ Read Matthew 12:36
○ Read Hebrews 4:13
○ Read 1 John 3:4

# Where did sin come from?

Sin started way back
In the Garden of Eden
When Adam and Eve
Started eatin' and feedin'
On fruit that God told them
Was not to be chowed:
*"That fruit is forbidden!*
*No nibbling allowed!"*

But Eve went ahead
And she took some and bit it.
And Adam did, too
(But he wouldn't admit it).
And neither would she,
So as quick as can be,
They hid 'cause they knew
It was *sin* they'd committed!

*They both disobeyed!*
*Though they both knew it was wrong,*
*The two ate the fruit*
*When the snake came along!*

They were scared and ashamed
And all guilty inside.
For they'd disobeyed God,
And they wanted to hide!
But God knew where they were,
And He knew what they'd done,
And He knew that they'd found out
That sin is no fun!
    (Though it seems at the time
    Like a pretty safe bet,
    Sin always brings sadness
    And fear and regret.)

CHECK it out then CHECK it off...

○ Read Genesis 3:1-24
○ Read Romans 5:12

# What did God promise Adam and Eve?

With sinning came dying
And suffering and pains,
Decay and destruction
And sickness and stains.
Things rotting! Things stinking!
Things making a mess!
And Eve wearing leaves
For her shirt and her dress!
    (And Adam wore pants
    Made of plants, I would guess!)

They had to move out
And start living with hope.
They learned about sweat
And they learned about soap!
They faced the results
Of the choices they chose.
    *Yet God offered a promise
    And made them new clothes!*

For He still loved this couple,
So He promised to send
    A Son who would suffer
    Yet win in the end!
    He'd crush all the evil
    That led them astray—
    Their descendant would stomp
    On the tempter one day!

Yes, they'd have to adjust
To a world filled with pain,
But by trusting God's promise
They could one day obtain
A close friendship with God
Only *faith* can regain!

CHECK it out then CHECK it off...

○ Read Genesis 3:14, 15

## Does everyone sin?

What was true in the garden,
Is still true today.
We still choose to sin.
We still disobey.
We want what's forbidden.
We reach out and try it,
And then when we're caught,
We try hard to deny it!
The Bible says *all* of us
Drift into sin.
Yes, even *nice* people
Are sinful within!
    Bad thoughts,
    And bad words,
    And not doing what's right.
    From dawn until dusk!
    From morning 'til night!
Instead of admitting
And facing our shame
We hide and pretend,
Make excuses and blame!

All people are sinners,
And must be forgiven
For the sins that we do
And the lives that we're livin'!
For we're born with this longing
To sin deep inside us—
  Conceited and selfish
  Like greedy King Midas!

  But God still adores us,
  (It's hard to know why!)
  For we matter so much
  He was willing to die!
  And He's always nearby
  With a promise to share,
  With hope for all sinners!
  Anytime! Anywhere!

CHECK it out then CHECK it off...

○ Read Romans 3:23

# Do I need to be forgiven?

Sin makes our God sad
'Cause He's holy and pure.
And just like a disease,
There is only one cure
To get rid of your sin—
You can't just ignore it,
And never, no never,
Embrace or adore it!
Sin can't be excused,
Overlooked, or denied.
It'll only grow stronger,
Increasing your pride!
It cannot be mended
Or patched up or fixed.
What is holy and sinful
Can never be mixed!

For sin is so serious,
God can't let it stay.
It must be forgiven
And taken away!
It must be removed,
And it must be replaced,
Discarded, departed,
Destroyed, and displaced!
   And instead of that *sin*,
   When we trust in God's grace,
   All the *good* deeds of Jesus
   Are heaped in its place!

CHECK it out then CHECK it off...

○ Read 1 John 1:8-10

# Why did Jesus have to die?

The sentence for sinning
Is dying, and so
All people will die
And eventually go
To a coffin or graveyard
Or burial site
'Cause we've all done what's wrong
And neglected what's right!

Now, God was aware
Of our hopeless condition,
And He loved us so much
That He gave His permission
For Jesus to live
And to die in our place.
　　(Not because we deserve it,
　　Just because of His grace!)

Jesus offered His life
As our sole substitution—
　　The ultimate,
　　Only salvation solution!

By suffering the punishment
That we all deserved,
And by taking our place,
God's justice was served.
There was no other way
For our debt to be paid,
And there's no way repaying
The love He displayed!

Now, all the wrong things
That we think, do, or say,
Every one of those wrongs
Has been taken away!
And the way to receive
All He offers to us,
Is to simply believe.
Surrender.
And trust.

CHECK it out then CHECK it off...

○ Read John 3:16
○ Read Romans 3:25

# What should I remember about sin?

So to sum up the story
and explain it all briefly:

*"All people still sin.*
*We choose sinning quite chiefly.*
*For instead of pursuing*
*The things that we ought,*
*We do what we shouldn't*
*In word, deed, and thought.*
*And the problem's so big*
*It's beyond comprehension!*
*Without any help*
*We'd be stuck in the tension*
*Of hopelessly hoping*
*For God's intervention!*

*"But God solved the problem*
*The day Jesus died.*
*We don't need to run.*
*We don't have to hide.*
*We can trust God's forgiveness.*
*It's completed and done.*
*God saved us from sin*
*By the death of his Son."*

CHECK it out then CHECK it off...

○ Read Romans 3:23, 24

# Can't I get into heaven by being good?

Most people just try
To make up for their wrongs
By doing good deeds,
Or singing some songs.
They think they're impressive
When they give advice—
    "Be caring. Be thoughtful.
    Be moral. Be nice.
    Do your best! Follow rules!
    And try hard to be good!
    Go to church! And obey!
    And do just what you should!
    Do more right than wrong.
    Do more good than bad.
    And you'll earn life in heaven
    And God will be glad!"

But that's *not* good advice!
God isn't a fool!
He knows every time
That we've broken a rule!
     And He won't be impressed
     By a bunch of good deeds.
     (Or even reciting
     The coolest of creeds!)
For the best we can do
Is never enough.
By ourselves we can't wash off
This filthy sin-stuff!
The road into heaven isn't wide;
No, it's slim.
For Jesus said the only way in
Is through Him!
     That's the news you must either
     Refuse or receive.
     Heaven *only* is open
     To those who believe!

CHECK it out then CHECK it off...

○ Read Ephesians 2:8, 9

## Are heaven and hell real places?

We each have a body
That grows and gets sturdier,
Getting more and more handsome,
Or more and more purttier.
    (So it's easier for teens
    To get more and more flirtier!)
Our bodies get bigger.
Our muscles mature.
Our hair may get longer.
It may look like fur!
    But the body you see
    Isn't all that exists.
    There's a *soul* inside
    That won't die, but persists.

Our bodies wear out.
They don't last forever.
But our souls will not die.
Not tomorrow. Not ever.
    When you die you just change
    The place where you dwell
    From here on the earth
    Into heaven or hell.

It's hard to imagine,
Admit, and to know,
But we're not here forever.
Someday we will go
Up to heaven above,
Or to hell down below!

Wherever you've traveled
Or flown through the sky
There are only two places
To go when you die.
Either heaven or hell.
Just two places only.
With God you'd be happy,
Without Him it's lonely.
　　With moanings and groanings
　　Most moanly and groanly!

CHECK it out then CHECK it off...

○ Read Matthew 25:31-46

# What will heaven be like?

Won't heaven be boring,
Just singing all day,
Or strumming a harp,
And learning to pray?
    No, heaven's not boring!
    Not ever! It's cool!
    It's not like a lecture
    You sit through at school!

It's more like a playground
Than sitting in class,
    Or a great slumber party. . .
    That lasts. . . and lasts. . .

With dancing and singing
And laughter and fun!
And the party in heaven
Will *never* be done!

With joy beyond knowing
And peace without end
And playing with God
Like you'd play with a friend!
It's a great celebration!
A joyful occasion!
A family reunion
All Christians attend!
And God will be waiting
With arms open wide
To welcome you home
And invite you inside.
With a smile on His face
And a room with a view,
"Welcome home," He will whisper.
"I've been waiting for you."

CHECK it out then CHECK it off...

 ○ Read Revelation 21:1-4

# What does it mean to be a Christian?

We believe in the message
Of what God has done;
And confess that our faith
Is in Jesus, His Son.
We love God and offer Him
All of our praise,
As we're putting Him first
And pursuing His ways!
    We give Him the glory,
    We trust in His story,
    And our hope
    Helps us cope
    During difficult days!

We're baptized and know
That our lives are renewed;
And we grow in our faith,
When the news is reviewed!
For we know that the Spirit
Works faith in the heart.
That He gives us new life
And He grants a fresh start.

On our own all alone
We couldn't know how to choose it.
We would never believe.
We would want to refuse it.
For sinners are stubborn! We need to be sought,
So God sends His Spirit and sinners are brought!
(Kinda like fish in a net that are caught!)

Yes, the Spirit draws us in,
And He helps us confess,
The best word of all.
The simple word, "Yes!"

*"Yes! I'm a sinner. I've done what is bad,*
*Yes! I want God as my heavenly Dad,*
*Yes! I believe Jesus paid for my sin,*
*Yes, I say! Yes, today! God, come on in!"*
(It isn't the words or the way that we say 'em;
But because we believe as we read and we pray 'em!)

So we're saved by the grace
Of the God that we love
And can't wait for our place
Up in heaven above!

CHECK it out then CHECK it off...

○ Read Psalm 86:12
○ Read Matthew 6:33
○ Read Acts 2:38
○ Read Romans 10:9

# What happens when I become a Christian?

When God's Holy Spirit
Comes in to reside.
In a flash you're renewed
From within the inside!
From lost into found!
From darkness to light!
From zero to hero,
Despair to delight!
From dead to alive!
From stranger to friend!
From life without hope
To a life without end!

And to remind you of who
You became on that day,
Here is a great little rhyme
You can say:

*"Now I'm*
*Saved like a swimmer*
*Who's snatched from a shark!*
*Guided with light*
*From above through the dark!*
*Rescued! I'm rescued!*
*My soul cannot die!*
*My cocoon life is over,*
*I'm learning to fly!*

*"For my sins are forgiven!*
*Forgotten! And gone!*
*As far as the dark*
*From the sun in the dawn!*
*Erased and deleted*
*And pulled from the stack.*
*They're vanished! And dropped*
*Down a bottomless crack!*
*There's no more rewinding,*
*And no more reminding.*
*My wrongs are long gone*
*And they cannot come back!"*

CHECK it out then CHECK it off...

○ Read 2 Corinthians 5:17

# Does God forgive me even if I don't say I'm sorry?

The forgiveness of God
Is a deal that's done.
It doesn't depend
On reciting each one
Of the things you've done wrong
Or the things you regret.
    (That list would be
    Longer than long I would bet!)

No, it doesn't depend
On how well you remember
The mistakes that you made
Sometime last December.

Don't think of forgiveness
As something you *do*.
It cannot be earned,
Only *offered* to you.
　　And it isn't the words
　　That you mumble or shout,
　　But the change in your heart
　　That brings it about!

For a Christian,
Confessing need never be clever.
God said you're not guilty
For now and forever.
You're part of His family.
You're His. You belong,
Even if you can't list
Every thing you've done wrong!

CHECK it out then CHECK it off...

○ Read Hebrews 10:14

# Can I be sure I'll go to heaven?

Heaven is certain
When faith is for real.
No matter how lousy
Or great you may feel.
For it doesn't rely
On you "doing your part."
God said He won't leave you.
He'll never depart!

Though you may have some bad times
Or sad times or doubt,
Your home is in heaven—
He won't kick you out!

Rely on His promise.
Lean on His grace.
He's forgiven your sins
And reserved you a place.
Once you're name's in His book,
He won't ever erase it!
He won't cross it out,
Or forget, or misplace it.
From the moment God's Spirit
Gives you life that is new,
    (From the faith that you have,
    Not the deeds that you do)
From that moment on,
Yes, from that very day,
Every one of your sins
Has been taken away!
    Being saved is forever!
    It's secure and decreed!
    It's a promise one hundred percent
    Guaranteed!

CHECK it out then CHECK it off...

○ Read Hebrews 13:5
○ Read Romans 8:1

# What should I remember about sin and salvation?

Though we might have our highs
And we might have our lows,
And we might disobey
From our head to our toes;
God isn't surprised
By the wrongs that we do,
He made us and knows
When we're bad
Through and through.
    Yet the bad thoughts we think,
    And the bad words we say,
    And the bad things we do,
    Jesus took them away.

For Christians believe
That the wrongs we have done
Are forgiven and paid for
By Jesus, God's Son.

So here is the secret,
To sum it up nicely.
Remember these words
And their message precisely:
*"Heaven never depends*
*On the deeds that you do,*
    *But the faith that you have*
    *In what God did for you!"*

CHECK it out then CHECK it off...

○ Read Ephesians 2:8-10

# Part 7

Living as a
Christian

## What is prayer?

Some folks fold their hands,
Others kneel or lay,
And some close their eyes
When they worship or pray.
But the *how* is not as vital
As *who* we hold dear.
We must pray believing.
We must be sincere.
For praying is talking
With our heavenly Father.
He never minds listening.
It's never a bother.
And He hears every prayer.
Not a few. Not just some.
And He answers all prayers,
No matter how dumb.

Sometimes God says "no"
To the things we request,
But the truth is,
God always allows what is best!
So remember this saying,
Down to the last letter:
*God'll give what you ask for*
*Or something much better!*

CHECK it out then CHECK it off...

○ Read Philippians 4:6
○ Read 1 John 5:14, 15

# What should I pray for?

We can thank God for all
Of the blessings He sends.
We can pray for the needs
Of our family and friends.
We can ask Him to heal people
Hurting or sick,
To help 'em get better
And cure 'em up quick!
　　We can ask for forgiveness
　　And tell Him we're sorry
　　And trust in the promises
　　Found in His story!
We can even tell God
When we're angry or sad,
And be glad that He listens
Without getting mad!

But prayer is much more
Than just mumbling words!
It's honoring God
With the praise He deserves.
So by serving Him daily
And making wise choices,
We can pray with our *lives*
As well as our *voices!*

CHECK it out then CHECK it off...

○ Read Matthew 6:9-13

# What is the armor of God?

Fighting daily temptation
Is like fighting a war!
But don't worry,
God gives us protection galore!
*Truth* acts like a belt
That holds up your pants
When you run or you jump
Or you climb or you dance.
    (So lies cannot trick you
    If given the chance!)
God's *righteousness* helps us
To do what is right,
And protects us from evil
By day and by night.

While the *good news of peace*
Helps us always be ready
To go where God leads us,
Or stand firm and steady.
Our *faith* is a shield
That protects from attack.
   (Like toothpaste that guards
   Your little toothies from plaque!)
And *salvation* is a helmet
That helps us to know
That we're certainly saved
Wherever we go.
   While *God's Word in the Bible*
   Is as sharp as a sword,
   Cutting through our excuses,
   Revealing the Lord;
   Defending God's promises,
   Showing they're true;
   And fighting off evil
   In all that we do!
Add *prayer*, and you're ready
For the brawl to begin
As you fight for what's right
Against evil and sin!

CHECK it out then CHECK it off...

○ Read Ephesians 6:11-18

## What does it mean to have faith?

You trust in a chair
Every time you sit down,
If the chair wasn't there,
Then you'd plop on the ground!
    (And if it were broken,
    It wouldn't be great,
    But you'd sit if you thought
    It would hold up your weight!)
You trust that the stars
And the moon and the air,
Still exist even when
You can't see them up there.
And you trust in the water
You get from the sink—
If you didn't, you wouldn't go
Reach for a drink!

If you know you can't swim,
You won't jump in a lake,
*For the things you believe*
*Change the actions you take.*

And your choices depend
On the trust that you give,
So the things you believe
Shape the life that you live!

Now, Christians have faith
That our God is for real.
And it's not just a wish
Or a feeling we feel.
For faith is believing in
What you can't see.
And it's not about proof,
Because trust is the key.
So we trust in a God
Who we love and won't leave,
And we base our whole lives
On these things we believe.

CHECK it out then CHECK it off...

○ Read Hebrews 11:1

# How can I grow in my faith?

We grow in our faith
By worship and prayer,
By studying Scripture,
And showing we care,
By sharing the message
That Jesus has won,
And by thinking about
All the things He has done.

> By learning and trusting
> And loving and giving,
> We're letting God's love
> Change the way that we're living.
> So that each night as daylight
> Begins to grow dim,
> We can know that we've grown
> Just a bit more like Him!

Step by step you keep growing,
Though it's noticed by no one.
For the process of growing
Your faith is a slow one.
Don't rush it. Be patient.
No pretending or stopping.
No fizzling out
Or fading or flopping.
Let God be your guide
As you learn how to trust.
　　And just ask Him to help you
　　Whenever you must!

God is pleased when your faith
Just continues to grow
From ideas you've heard,
　　To ideas you know,
　　Into actions you simply
　　Can't help but to show!

CHECK it out then CHECK it off...

○ Read Colossians 2:6, 7

# Can I say "no" to sin?

Sin loses its grip
When we hold onto Jesus.
He strengthens our faith.
And He rescues and frees us
So we can say "no"
When temptations appear,
And we can face Satan
Without any fear!
For Jesus has taken
His power away
And sent us the Spirit
To help us today!

Now, we'll never be perfect—
We still fail and fall.
Thinking thoughts that we
Ought not to think of at all.
Doing deeds that are naughty.
Saying things that are mean.
But Jesus forgives us!
He's there on the scene!

And one by one we can change
The wrong habits we've had,
So that through faith we're doing
What's good and not bad!

CHECK it out then CHECK it off...

○ Read James 4:7

# Do I have to be good all the time?

Here's some news that might sound
Like it shouldn't be true:
*Christians don't have to do*
*What God tells them to do!*
Now, don't get me wrong
Or confuse what I say.
The secret I'm sharing
Shouldn't lead you astray—
The point is we *get to*,
Not *have to* obey!
Obeying is kinda like
A gift that we give
'Cause we're thankful to God
For the new life we live.

So our future is hopeful,
Not grave and not grim,
As we slowly grow more and more
Pleasing to Him.
Choosing right over wrong
Is not a game that we play.
We just want to be more
Like our Hero each day!
We act like He wants
And we do what we should.
Not to try to impress Him,
We just *like* being good!
(And it brings Him more pleasure
Than wrongdoing would!)

CHECK it out then CHECK it off...

○ Read John 14:15
○ Read John 14:21
○ Read John 14:23

# Do I need to keep the Ten Commandments?

God gave Ten Commandments
As a guide for our lives,
So here's how to act
Until He arrives:

1. Only worship the true God,
   The one God alone.
2. Don't ever make idols
   Of plastic or stone.
3. Use God's name with honor
   And use it with care.
4. Take one day a week
   For worship and prayer.
5. Always honor your parents.
   Respect and obey 'em.
6. Don't harm other people
   Or murder or slay 'em!
7. Be loyal in marriage,
   Avoiding affairs.
8. Don't steal things from others
   Or take what is theirs.
9. Don't lie or deceive
   Or say things that aren't true.
10. And don't scheme to get
    What's not given to you.

Should you keep 'em?
Yes, keep 'em!
And carry 'em around!
In your head and your heart
They should always be found.
But why should you keep 'em?
What good does it do?

*It's a way to show thanks*
*For what God's done for you!*

CHECK it out then CHECK it off...

○ Read Exodus 20:1-17

# Why does God let bad things happen?

When boys give you cooties
Or girls give you germs,
And you feel like going
And eating some worms,
When nothing goes right
And you just want to yelp—
Where's God? What's He doing?
Why doesn't He help?

Sometimes life is painful.
Sometimes we may doubt.
Sometimes God allows things
We can't figure out.

But God has a plan
That He's carefully weaving
To bless those who love Him
And keep on believing.
He's still in control.
Don't be gloomy or glum.
He's promised us justice
And good things to come.
    So, the times that we suffer
    Are the times we must trust
    That God is still there
    And He's caring for us.

CHECK it out then CHECK it off...

○ Read Matthew 5:4

# Part 8

# The Church and Its Practices

# What is baptism?

Baptism's a picture
Or a way that you show
That your faith is in God
And you want it to grow!

It's not magic spells
Or some kind of a potion,
Like "Abra-cadabra-calabra-calotion!"
It's not hocus pocus,
Or "Ala-kazeaven!"
Baptism alone will not
Get you to heaven.

The Bible says baptism
Washes off sin—
But not like the dirt
That you get on your skin—
    For that's on the outside
    And not on the in;
    And baptism's a way
    Of scrubbing within!

Going under the water
Might seem kind of odd,
But it's like a short play
You act out before God!
  Just think of the grave
  That Jesus went in—
  All cold and alone
  Because of your sin.
  He came out alive
  And the new life He had
  Made people united, excited, and glad!

Going under the water
Is like *burying your sin*.
Your old life is gone!
You have new life within!
And when you come up,
Then you show that it's clear—
That the old you is gone
And the new you is here!
  It's like Easter again!
  And it's God's invitation
  To show that you're part
  Of the great celebration!

CHECK it out then CHECK it off...

○ Read Matthew 3:13-16
○ Read Romans 6:3, 4

# Why should I be baptized?

If you like a sports hero,
You might wear a hat
Of the team he plays for,
Or something like that.
You might buy a jersey
Or coat from the store
To show other people
Whose team you adore.
You wouldn't be frightened
Or ashamed if they knew.
You'd want them to know
Who's a hero to you!

Well, baptism shows that
Your hero is Jesus!
Who came to restore,
Renew, and release us!

Jesus said to be baptized!
So that's why we do it!
His disciples were baptized
Because they all knew
It was what Jesus wanted,
And so they obeyed!
And it *still* is important.
So don't be afraid!

    If you trust in Christ
    And want others to know it,
    Step up and get baptized!
    It's the best way to show it!

CHECK it out then CHECK it off...

○ Read Mark 16:16

# What is the Lord's Supper?

There's more to this supper
Than eating and drinking.
It's a way for your brain
And your heart to start thinking
About the sad night
When our Lord was betrayed,
And about the great price
That His sacrifice paid.
For after they'd eaten,
Jesus spoke up and said,

> "Take and drink from this cup.
> Take and eat of this bread.
> The wine is my blood
> To forgive what you do.
> And the bread is my body
> That's broken for you."

On the one hand it's sad,
And you may feel like crying
'Cause this meal is a way
To remember His dying.
    But it's also a way
    To celebrate His achievement
    'Cause He opened up heaven
    For those with *believement!*
    And now, as we gather
    To taste of the mystery,
    We thankfully share
    All that's brother and sisterly
    'Cause we're part of a family
    That's part of His history!

CHECK it out then CHECK it off...

&#9675; Read Matthew 26:26-28
&#9675; Read Acts 2:42

# What is The Church?

The biggest Church ever
Isn't built out of stone
Or metal or plastic
Or concrete or foam.
It doesn't have walls
And a roof and a door
Or windows or tile
Or a carpeted floor.
It doesn't have pews
Or even a steeple
'Cause this is the only Church
Built out of *people*!

(*I know it sounds leaky
In rainy, wet weather,
But the people aren't stapled
Or nailed together*!)

This Church is so special
'Cause it isn't a place—
It's simply the people
Aware of God's grace!
For they all trust in Jesus
And no longer search.
Their home is in heaven,
But while here, they're the Church!
All joined by their faith!
Like bricks in a wall—
   Wide ones and skinny ones;
   Short ones and tall,
All working together
So others may learn
That they matter to God
And He's gonna return!

CHECK it out then CHECK it off...

○ Read Ephesians 2:19-22

Our job is quite simple.
We simply proclaim
The message God gave us—
It's always the same:
*Our God loved the world*
*So much that He came*
*And died so that those*
*Who believe in the name*
*Of Jesus can have their sins*
*Taken away—*
> *Getting hope for tomorrow*
> *And peace for today!*

It's a message we want
Other people to know,
So we sum up our job
With the little word, "Go!"

Go and tell neighbors
And sisters and brothers.
Tell family and friends!
Tell fathers and mothers
And teachers and bullies
And Grandma and Gramps!
Go and tell strangers
And hobos and tramps,
And lawyers and plumbers
And athletes and kings
About the forgiveness
That only God brings!

Step out of your church
With its hymnals and pews,
And build up *the Church*
By sharing *the news*
With people close by
And those far, far away
So that more may believe
In God's message today!

CHECK it out then CHECK it off...

○ Read Matthew 28:18-20

## What kind of church should I go to?

There are so many churches!
Some big and some small.
Some old and some new.
Some short and some tall.
Some churches have organs,
And others have drums.
    (There may even be churches
    Where everyone hums!)
But no matter how nice
And no matter how crumbly,
The best churches always
Have members who humbly
    Believe what God tells them,
    And offer Him praise,
    And live to love others
    And follow His ways.

Church names may be different,
But our mission's the same:
*To tell about Jesus*
*And the reason He came.*
*That He planned out a plot,*
*And He plotted a plan*
*To remove all our sins*
*By becoming a man,*
*By dying and rising*
*And offering grace,*
*To reach out and rescue*
*The whole human race!*

That's the truth that we know
And the truth that we teach.
That's the news that God
Wants every pastor to preach.
If a pastor won't preach it,
Then something is wrong.
If a church will not teach it,
Then you don't belong.
Don't stay there a day!
Don't give it a thought!
Go find a new church
Where the Bible is taught!

CHECK it out then CHECK it off...

○ Read Galatians 1:8-10

# Why are there so many different kinds of churches?

It's helpful to know
We don't always agree.
I might argue with you,
You might argue with me
    As we search out the truth
    That God wants us to know
    And look through the Bible
    To learn how to grow.

So, churches are different.
Their teachings may vary.
And sometimes their views
May look very contrary!
It's easy to argue,
To blame, or get mad.
But don't be discouraged
Or angry or sad.

God wants us together
And never apart.
So keep this reminder
Close by in your heart:
    The things that divide us
    Are tiny compared
    To the truths that unite us
    In the love that He shared.
    For His love keeps us close
    And His love keeps us strong.
    Even during those days when
    We don't get along.

CHECK it out then CHECK it off...

○ Read 1 Peter 3:8

# What should I remember about the Church?

The Church needs a leader
To get the job done,
And the Church's one leader
Is Jesus, God's Son!
('Cause God is the boss
Of this Church you can't see—
This Church made of people
Like you and like me.)
But each local church
Plays a part in the mission
Of fishin' for souls
With its own style of fishin'!

Converting! Encouraging!
Equipping and sending!
Teaching, baptizing,
And always befriending!
It's exciting to see
The Church working today,
Using buildings where people
Can worship and pray!

*Yes, the Church uses buildings,*
*But always remember*
*It's faith, not attendance,*
*That makes you a member!*

CHECK it out then CHECK it off...

○ Read Ephesians 1:22-23

# Part 9

# God's Promises for the Future

# Does anyone know the future?

We don't know the future,
Our brains are restricted.
But God knows the future
And He can predict it!
He planned it and knows
What He's going to allow,
And He's chosen to give us
A glimpse of it now!

> *(In the Bible He gives us*
> *These hints and predictions,*
> *So we know they're all true*
> *And not fables or fictions!)*

As years pass us by
And time slips away,
The end of the age
Gets closer each day.
And just like a puddle
Growing wetter and wetter,
Things are gonna get worse
Before they get better!
For sorrow won't stop,
And sin will not cease,
And wickedness, sadness,
And pain will increase
As each new disaster
Makes clearer and clearer—
The end of the world
Is getting nearer and nearer!
*These things will all happen*
*Not to frighten or scare us,*
*But to warn and alert*
*And inform and prepare us!*

CHECK it out then CHECK it off...

○ Read Matthew 24:6-14
○ Read Matthew 24:36

# What will happen to Christians?

We don't need to worry
Or fret or be grievers,
For Christ will preserve
And will rescue believers!
When the time is just right,
He'll suddenly snatch
All Christians to heaven
In one giant batch!
We'll lift from the ground
And float up to the sky!
It's the only time ever
That people will fly!

Now, we don't know just when,
On what day, or what year—
But we do know that then
There'll be nothing to fear,
For we'll all be with Jesus
And no longer here!
    And there by the throne
    Where the Lord rules and leads,
    King Jesus will judge
    All our choices and deeds.
    And the faithful deeds done
    While back on the earth
    Will earn lasting treasures
    Of heavenly worth!

So the message God gives us
Is quite crystal clear:
    *Store treasures in heaven*
    *By serving Him here!*

CHECK it out then CHECK it off...

○ Read Matthew 6:19
○ Read Romans 2:5-8
○ Read 1 Thessalonians 4:15-17

# What will happen to unbelievers?

The future for Christians
Is bright and it's cheery,
But for all unbelievers
The future is dreary.
For Christians go up
And all others go down.
Christians will smile.
All others will frown.
    And Christians will join up
    With God's only Son,
    But everyone else
    Will be far from the fun.

For with no faith in Jesus,
Without Him within,
When God sees their lives
All He sees is their sin.
So they'll be sent from God,
From His love, and His peace
To a place of great pain
Without hope of release.

For sin must be punished,
Just like God has said,
So those without Christ
Won't enjoy what's ahead.
Their wrongs are recorded,
So when deeds are reported,
They won't be rewarded,
But will suffer instead.

CHECK it out then CHECK it off...

○ Read Romans 2:8, 9
○ Read Revelation 20:11-15

# What should I remember about the future?

So what happens after
The Judgment is through?
God will make a new sky
And a new planet, too!
For someday in place
Of the world that is here,
God'll make a pure,
Wonderful,
New one appear!
    Where no one gets sick
    And no one gets eaten.
    Where nothing will break
    And Satan's been beaten!
    And nothing can harm
    Or defeat or destroy
    God's kingdom of love
    And of gladness and joy!

Then Jesus will rule
As the King of all kings
Without sin or sadness
Or any such things.
No pain and no sickness.
No death whatsoever!
Just joy and great love
Getting better forever!

We know that it's coming.
It'll someday be here.
The future is certain.
God's promise is clear!

CHECK it out then CHECK it off...

 ○ Read Revelation 21:1-4

# Conclusion

We've covered the gamut,
The spectrum, and scope—
From sin to salvation,
Rebellion to hope.
It's the best news you'll ever
Retell or recall:
> *God loves us and offers*
> *Forgiveness to all!*

Now remember this line,
It's the last and the latest—
> *Our God is so great*
> *That our God is the greatest!*